LIVING
in the
FULLNESS
of the
Blessing

JERRY SAVELLE

Living in the Fullness of the Blessing
ISBN-13: 978-0-9702911-9-6
ISBN-10: 0-9702911-9-1

Jerry Savelle Ministries
P.O. Box 748
Crowley, TX 76036

CONTENTS

INTRODUCTION

While sitting in the back of my airplane, I was reading my Bible and looking over some notes of what I felt that I might be preaching at the Convention I was flying to. As I was doing that, the Lord instructed me to turn in my notebook to a prophetic word that Kenneth Copeland had given during the West Coast Believer's Convention.

The Lord said to me, "I want you to take that prophetic word and look at it and study it very closely because it has everything to do with what I am about to do in your life and the lives of those who would dare believe for it."

I took out the prophesy and began reading it over and over. I took out my highlighter and started highlighting certain things that seemed to stand out to me. I sensed in my spirit the Holy Spirit had something exciting that He wanted to reveal to me about the things which I had highlighted.

This is what the prophetic word said:

"The manifestation of the blessing, saith the Lord, is at an all time high. You are approaching a blessing manifestation that the human race has never seen before. The blessing will surround you. The blessing will encase you. All debt will have to get up and leave you the same way lep-

rosy left the lepers of old. Debt is financial sickness. It is financial leprosy. It is a burden and it is part of the curse. If you will begin to confess that this blessing manifestation is coming, you will be shocked and thrilled at how quickly you will have the glory arise and drive the debt right out of your life. I will bless you beyond your income. I will bless you beyond your salaries. I will bless you beyond anything you have ever known before. I will bring financial blessing on you that you don't have any idea where it came from. It has come to an explosive place. It's ready and I'm ready. Are you ready? Saith the Lord."

Did you notice what the Holy Spirit said about the "manifestation of the blessing like never before"?

I have often said that if the Lord did not do one more thing for me as long as I live, I could die and go to heaven and say without reservation that God has been good to Jerry Savelle. But it sounds as if the best is yet to come!

But did you know that for God not to do anything else for me (and you) would be contrary to His nature. Why? Because God is good and He is the God who increases us more and more. God really has no problem with how much you increase, just as long as He gets the credit for it (Deuteronomy 8:18).

Ever since the day I discovered that I had a right to be blessed by God, that I had a right to the blessing of Abraham, it absolutely changed my life. And I believe that once you understand what the blessing is and why you need to live in the fullness of it, then you will never be the same either. That is why I have written this book. The Lord has shared with me some keys to living in the fullness of the blessing. And if there is ever a time that you and I need to be living in the fullness of the blessing, it's today.

I hope you will take the principles in this book and apply them to your life. And when you do, I believe that the words of that prophecy will become a reality in your life.

God is ready for you to live in the fullness of His blessing. Are you daring enough to believe for it? I am. And I am ready to live it. Are you?

CHAPTER 1

THE FULLNESS OF THE BLESSING

Can you imagine what your life would be like right now if you had the ability to flow in God's blessing without measure? Live a life without any limitations? What would you be doing? How would you be living?

Did you know that God has provided a way for you to live a life without any limits. That's right. No limits.

Now you might be thinking, "But how, Jerry? What are you talking about?"

God has provided for you to live a life without limitations by pronouncing His blessing on your life. That's the kind of life He wants you to live. And that is why I have written this book. God wants you to live everyday in the fullness of the blessing that He has pronounced on you!

BE BLESSED

Not too long ago, my seven year old grandson and I were out in my garage working on his little Honda 50 dirt bike, getting it ready for him to ride. As we were working, he sneezed. I heard him but really didn't pay that much attention. I just kept working.

When I didn't say anything to him, he noticed. He got up, walked over, and put his hands on his hips and said, "Papa, you didn't empower me to prosper." I said, "Well, excuse me. Empower you to prosper."

I know you might be reading this and thinking, "What? Empower you to prosper? That doesn't make any sense. Why didn't you say what most people say: God bless you?"

I know that's what most people say. And unfortunately, that is probably about the only time the word "bless" is used in most Christian homes. Somebody sneezes and somebody else says: bless you. That's about the depth of their revelation of blessing.

But not at my house. I discovered over 35 years ago that one of the meanings of the word *bless* is *empowered to prosper.* So I just made that a habit at our house. If somebody sneezed, I would say, "empower you to prosper." And now I have taught that same thing to my grandkids. We believe in *the* blessing at our house.

The fact of the matter is that I wouldn't have anything if it wasn't for the blessing of God on my life. *The blessing* is an empowerment that comes on your life when you get born again. That's right! It comes on you. You wear it just like you wear your clothes. It's on you. It's not your car, it's not your house, and it's not your spouse. All of those things are by-products of *the blessing*, the empowerment that is on your life to prosper.

Genesis 1:26-27 – *And God said, Let us make man in our own image, after our likeness: and let them have dominion over the fish of the sea, and over the fowl of the air, and over the cattle, and over all the earth, and over every creeping thing that creepeth upon the earth. So God created man in his own image . . .*

And then in verse 28, it says – *And God blessed them . . .*

Notice that God created man and the first thing that He did after creating man was bless him.

Now how does God bless someone? How did He bless Adam? How did it take place? In the literal Hebrew, it implies that when God blessed Adam, it was something He pronounced on Him. He spoke it.

The very first words Adam ever heard God speak were, "Be blessed." That is amazing to me. You know, my Mom and Dad didn't say that to me right after I was born. My Dad didn't look at me and say, "Jerry Savelle, be blessed."

But those were the first words that Adam ever heard from God. Be blessed.

Once God pronounced the blessing on Adam, it came on him and he wore it like a coat. It was on him and it was on him in its fullness. Not a measure. The fullness of the blessing. The blessing was on him, and it had the ability to do things in his life and cause his lifestyle to be one without measure and without limits.

Because God had blessed Adam, he was marked. The blessing had been pronounced upon him and he was empowered to prosper, empowered to succeed. Before he committed high treason against God, Adam didn't know anything about failure. He was not designed to fail. He was designed to succeed.

And so are you. You were created in God's image just like Adam was. You were created to be blessed. You were created to succeed.

NOT ONLY ADAM

Just because Adam and Eve sinned, God's plan for mankind did not change. God started all over with a man by the name of Noah.

*And God blessed Noah and his sons, and said unto them,
Be fruitful, and multiply, and replenish the earth.*
— Genesis 9:1

Notice that these are the exact same words that God spoke
to Adam. In some translations it even says that God pronounced a blessing upon Noah and his sons. Noah was
blessed just like Adam was.

And what about Abram?

And I will make of thee a great nation and I will bless thee.
— Genesis 12:2

Abram was blessed just like Adam and Noah. He was
empowered to prosper and succeed. And if you study
Abraham's life, you will see that everywhere he went, and
everything that he did, produced increase. All he had to do
was walk in obedience.

*And Abraham was old, and well stricken in age; and the
Lord had blessed Abraham in all things.*
— Genesis 24:1

In other words, you could say that by the time Abraham
became an old man, he had experienced increase in ev-

ery area of his life. Increase had come to him in everything that he did. Why? Because he was blessed by God. The blessing had been pronounced upon him and it was noticeable.

YOUR TIME HAS COME

And if ye be Christ's, then ye are Abraham's seed, and heirs according to the promise.

– Galatians 3:29

That's you and me. We are Abraham's seed. If you belong to Christ, if you have accepted Him and made Him Lord of your life, then you are Abraham's seed.

You are a seed of Abraham and an heir according to the promise. God has pronounced His blessing upon you. It is time for you to walk in the fullness of that blessing.

The Lord hath been mindful of us: he will bless us; he will bless the house of Israel; he will bless the house of Aaron. He will bless them that fear the Lord, both small and great.

– Psalm 115:12-13

The Lord shall increase you more and more. Why? Because you're blessed of the Lord who made heaven and earth.

WHY YOU NEED THE BLESSING

Have you noticed how crazy the world has gotten? It's crazy out there. I don't know how people make it on this planet without the blessing of God on their lives. And it just seems to be getting worse as the days go by. But thank God for the blessing.

You see, when the blessing is on your life, you are not limited like other people. You are not limited to the natural any more. You have something working for you that other people don't have. It doesn't matter what is going on in your life. It doesn't matter what the circumstances are telling you. God has pronounced His blessing on you. He has empowered you to prosper and empowered you to succeed. He doesn't intend for you to fail. He has already placed the blessing on your life. He has already planned for your increase and your success.

Living in the fullness of the blessing is all about living a life without limitations. I believe that God wants each and every one of His children to live in the fullness of the blessing that He has pronounced on their lives. And God has shared with me some things that I believe will put you in position to live in the fullness of His blessing. No matter how blessed your life has been up until now, God has more for you. There is another level of the blessing that He wants you to walk in. I believe that the blessing manifestation is going to be far beyond anything that we have ever seen before. God is ready for you to live in the fullness of His blessing that He has pronounced on our life. Are you?

CHAPTER 2

STRETCH YOUR THINKING

The manifestation of the blessing is at an all time high. You are approaching a blessing manifestation like the human race has never seen before.

THE FULLNESS OF THE BLESSING

Romans 15:29 says, *And I am sure that, when I come unto you, I shall come in the **fulness of the blessing** of the gospel of Christ.*

The word *fullness* means *complete or having reached the greatest level or highest degree.* That is the nature of God. He is always calling us up higher. He is always wanting us to go further. He is always progressing, and He is calling us up to a higher level.

GET OUT OF THE COMFORT ZONE

I have noticed in my life that it seems like God does not allow me to get in comfort zones. I never seem to reach the place where I can go, "Okay, I've arrived. Praise God." And then throw the armor in the corner and take a spiritual vacation. I never seem to get to the place where I don't have to use my faith.

The disciples of Jesus had some struggles from time to time. I mean the religious people hated them. Take Lazarus for example. Do you remember when they found out Lazarus was sick? Jesus waited for three days before He went to be with Lazarus and his family.

When Jesus finally told His disciples that they were going to go see him, they said, "But Master, don't you understand the last time we were in that city they tried to stone us?" He said, "Yes, I understand that." They said, "Well, if Lazarus is asleep, he is doing okay."

The disciples had rocks on their brain. The religious Jews were the best "rock chunkers" in the world. They didn't miss. When they stoned you, you were dead. And the disciples were thinking, "Man, the last time we were there, they wanted to throw rocks at us. Let's just stay here." But you see, Jesus wouldn't allow them to stay in their comfort zone. He was always stretching their faith.

And then there's the time on the Mount of Transfiguration. Peter, James, and John were with Jesus and the manifestation of the glory of God. What did they want to do? They wanted to build a tabernacle right there. Why? Because they'd have gotten in a comfort zone.

What about the children of Israel right after Moses died? They hated Moses when he was living, but when he died they just wanted to hang around and mourn his death. But God wouldn't let them stay in that comfort zone. He finally said, in the form of a rebuke, "Moses is dead. Now get up and go and take the land that I told you belongs to you."

Do you see what I am saying? God's people tend to want to just get comfortable sometimes. We tend to want to find that place where there's no resistance. But that's not what God wants. Right after you finish one faith project, God is already talking about stretching you for the next one. Go further. Go deeper. Expand. Build. Rise. God has got a one track mind, and it always involves increase.

God has told us that it's time for the manifestation of the blessing to be at an all time high. That means you and I are going to have to stretch our faith if we're going to become recipients of it. This is not going to happen to small thinking, negative talking Christians.

I want to encourage you to start confessing right now that you are headed for the fullness of the blessing in your life.

You must begin to confess it so that you take the limits off of your thinking. If you say it enough, you will eventually begin to believe it.

A MORE EXTRAVAGANT BLESSING

In the Message translation, it describes the fullness of the blessing as *a more extravagant blessing.* And the definition for the word *extravagant* is *going beyond any previous limits.* That simply means going to the next level. God is calling you and me to the next level of His blessing on our lives.

Now a lot of people don't like the word, extravagant, particularly religious people. Excessive, extravagant. The religious world has a hard time with this. But, God's the one who said it, so I'm going for it!

Ephesians 2:7 says, *That in the ages to come he might show the exceeding riches of his grace in his kindness toward us through Christ Jesus.*

Paul wrote this ages ago. But I have reason to believe that when Paul wrote this he was looking into the spirit realm, into the future and he saw our generation.

I've had people tell me, "No, he's talking about heaven."

Well, let me ask you something. Why would I need the exceeding riches of His grace and His kindness and His favor when I get to heaven? I'm not going to need them when I get to heaven. There are no problems in heaven. If you haven't heard, the devil isn't going.

I need the exceeding riches of His grace and His kindness and His favor while I'm in this place called earth. Heaven has been referred to as the sweet by and by. I'm not going to need this in the sweet by and by. I need it in the lousy here and now.

I believe when Paul wrote this, he saw you and me. I believe he was looking into the future and saw in the spirit a generation of believers who would be on planet Earth just before the appearing of Jesus and that group of people were going to experience God's grace, God's favor and God's kindness beyond anything any other generation had ever experienced. I believe that's our generation. I believe that's you and me.

IMMEASURABLE, LIMITLESS, AND SURPASSING

The Amplified says, (Ephesians 2:7) *He did this that He might clearly demonstrate through the ages to come the immeasurable (limitless, surpassing) riches of His free*

grace (His unmerited favor) in [His] kindness and good-
ness of heart toward us in Christ Jesus.

Doesn't that sound extravagant to you? Doesn't that sound
like the fullness of the blessing to you? And when is He
going to do this? When they get to heaven? No. I believe
He is intending to do this for a generation of people that
are living on planet Earth who will dare to believe Him for
it before the appearing of Jesus. I'm declaring by faith that
I'm going to walk in the fullness of the blessing before the
appearing of Jesus. How about you?

IT'S A SURE THING

I love what Paul said in Romans 15:29, *And I am sure
that, when I come unto you, I shall come in the fulness of
the blessing . . .*

I like a sure thing, don't you?

When God made His promises to Abraham (Hebrews 6:14)
regarding that blessing, He said, ***Surely** I will bless thee.
Surely I will multiply thee.* He didn't say maybe, perhaps,
there's a strong possibility. He said "It's a **sure** thing Abraham, I'm going to bless you."

Paul said, "I am **sure** that I am going to walk in this" (author's paraphrase). And I'm saying by faith, I am **sure** that

I am going to walk in the fullness of the blessing to the point that is immeasurable, limitless and surpassing anything I've ever experienced before. How about you?

Stop and think about it. We have a better covenant founded upon better promises, and if we don't go beyond what Abraham walked in, then what good is a new covenant? God wants us to go further than that. God wants us to surpass that.

AN EXPLOSIVE PLACE

It has come to an explosive place. It's ready. I'm ready. Get ready. Saith the Lord.

It's come to an explosive place. Do you know what that sounds like to me? A quick work.

I occasionally ride my motorcycle through Colorado, and I ride through many tunnels dug out of the mountains. Somebody had to carve through the rock to make those tunnels. How long do you suppose it would take to carve a tunnel with a hammer and a chisel? If that's how they had to do it, then they might still be working on it.

But if you want to get some stuff out of the way real quick, what do you do? You blow it up. One of the definitions for the word *explosion* is a *sudden, widespread increase.* And the words that the spirit of God chose I don't think are a coincidence. Explosive.

It goes right along with the word of God. In Haggai 2:6-8 it says, *The silver is mine and the gold is mine, and I'm going to shake it lose* (author's paraphrase). The quickest way to get gold and silver out of the hands of the wicked is to just blast it out of there. When God said the wealth of the sinner's been laid up for the just (Proverbs 13:22), He's not talking about them coming and giving us $50 at a time over a period of 9,000 years.

If the sinner still has it when we are supposed to have it before the appearing of Jesus, then the quickest way for God to get it out of their hands is shake it. And when you explode something, things get shaken. I am not talking about a physical explosion. I believe God is getting ready to cause a Spiritual explosion in the Earth called the blessing explosion.

Like I said earlier, one of the definitions for the word *explosion* is a *sudden, widespread increase.* One of my favorite words in the Bible is *suddenly.* I'm willing to stand and having done all to stand, stand. And believe me, over the last 39 years, I have become an expert in the art of standing. I know how to stand. But, when God starts doing things suddenly, I get excited.

CAN YOU IMAGINE?

Can you imagine planting a seed and before you get it out of your hand, the harvest is already there? That is a sudden, widespread increase!

"No, I can't imagine that Jerry." Well, then you're going to have to do some stretching in your thinking.

Why? Because not everybody in the body of Christ will experience living in the fullness of the blessing or the blessing explosion. Why? Because not everybody in the body of Christ will believe for it. Not everybody in the body of Christ will position themselves to receive it. And not everybody will be willing to stretch their thinking to the point that God can get it to them.

One of the things that I love about Oral Roberts is that he will not allow you to think small. I mean he absolutely refuses to allow you to think small. If you talk small to Oral Roberts, he will turn his head and won't even pay attention to you anymore.

He has on his desk a plaque that says, "No small plans made here."

He asked me one time if he could go to Africa with me. I told him that I was going to be extremely busy and would not have much time to spend with him, but if he wanted to go that was fine.

One of the reasons he wanted to go was because I was building a medical center, and his ministry was going to staff it with doctors and nurses who had graduated from Oral Roberts University.

We were building this medical center in an area where there was nearly two million people without any medical facilities. I was going over there to ask the President of that nation for land to build it on. And so, Brother Roberts goes with me.

Here we are sitting in this meeting with all these government officials, my staff, Brother Roberts, and me. They are addressing me and Oral Roberts. They are telling us how much they appreciate us coming and our project. I am listening just as attentively as I possibly can, and I look over and notice Oral Roberts has his head down and is writing on a napkin. He hasn't looked up since they greeted us. I am wondering what the problem is but still paying attention. He is scribbling something on a napkin. He then folds it up, throws it away, and gets another napkin. And finally right in the middle of the official's speech, Brother Roberts nudges me. I don't know whether to look at him or not. He nudges me again, and I look over at him and he hands me this napkin. He says, "Do you know what this says?" I looked at it. I said, "Brother Roberts, I do not have a clue what that says."

I looked back to make sure that the official knew that I was paying attention. Brother Roberts nudged me again. He said, "That's Oral Roberts spelled backwards." That's when I realized he' was not impressed with what was being said.

I said, "Brother Roberts, are we boring you here?"

He said, "Quite frankly, yes."

I said, "Why? Aren't you interested in what these people are saying?"

He said, "No."

"Why not?"

He said, "They think too small."

That trip taught me a something. I learned that when you are talking small, this man wouldn't even listen to you. He'd just turn you off. He'd just act like you were not even in the room.

That's about the way you and I are going to have to get if we're ever going to get into the fullness of the blessing. We're going to have to stop hanging around small talking, small thinking people. And we've got to quit thinking small and talking small ourselves. You need to get around people that will stretch you. Don't feel intimidated around big thinkers. Just don't open your mouth and they'll think you're one of them.

DON'T GET JEALOUS

The dumbest thing I have ever heard of is when people get jealous over somebody else increasing. Instead of getting jealous, you should be rejoicing. Why? Because it proves that it can be done. So instead of getting jealous, rejoice and thank God with them. Use their experience to stretch your faith and believe that it can happen for you.

God is calling you to a higher level. He is calling you to get out of your comfort zone and to stretch your thinking. He is calling you to live in the fullness of the blessing. Are you ready and willing to believe Him for it?

CHAPTER 3

FINANCIAL LEPROSY

And all debt will have to get up and leave you the same way leprosy left the lepers of old.

Debt leaving us like it left the lepers of old. That is an interesting thought to me. I had never heard anything quite like that before.

I asked the Lord, "Why did you make that kind of analogy?"

He said, "Debt is financial sickness. It is financial leprosy."

But I still wondered why He would compare it to leprosy.

He said, "Because it will eat away at your life. It will decay and destroy your life like leprosy. And just like the lepers of old, obviously they were restricted. They were confined. They couldn't even live in the city. They couldn't be around the rest of humanity which meant they had restrictions, confinements, and limitations."

And that is exactly what debt does to most people. It confines them. It limits them. It restricts them. And God called it financial leprosy.

I got out my Bible and my Strong's Concordance, and I looked up every scripture I could find on the subject of leprosy because I knew God had some revelation here. I knew He was not just playing with words.

IT WAS IN THEM

This is what I discovered. In nearly every reference to leprosy, the thing that interested me the most was it never said it was *on* them. It said it was *in* them.

I don't know why but always before, it seemed that when I would read through Matthew, Mark, Luke, and John, and I would watch Jesus minister to the lepers, I would think that it was *on* them. Leprosy was *on* them. But it doesn't say that. It says it was *in* them.

When the plague of leprosy is in a man . . .

– Leviticus 13:9

I began to notice that every time Jesus ministered to a leper, it would say, *and it departed out of them.* It didn't say it got off of them. Why? Because it wasn't *on* them. It was *in* them.

Now, it did affect their outward appearances. Leprosy could cause a part of your nose to be removed. It could cause a part of your ear to decay. It decayed the flesh.

You have probably seen the movies where they have shown lepers. You know, where they have gauze over their faces because it's hideous looking.

Even though leprosy affected them outwardly, it was not on them. It was in them. And isn't that what debt does? It can affect you outwardly, but it is not on you – it gets in you.

I asked the Lord, "Now, Lord, how does this parallel with debt?"

He said, "For most of my people, debt is not only on them; it's in them. They are not only in debt. Debt is in them. "

I said, "How did it get there?"

He said, "Training. Upbringing. Small thinking. Limiting themselves. Thinking that's the only way they can get something done."

Let me remind you here that one of the blessings of Abraham is: *Thou shalt lend to many and not borrow* (Deuteronomy 28:12).

I am not saying it is a sin to borrow. That's not what I am saying at all.

But what God is saying is that when the blessing is operating in you in its fullness, you won't have to borrow. You will be the lender.

YOU CAN DO THAT?

When Carolyn and I first started out we were broke. We didn't have any money. I didn't know people paid cash for anything. My Mom and Dad borrowed money all their lives. That was the only way I knew. Debt was in me.

I graduated from high school and the first thing my Dad did was introduce me to the Vice President of the bank. He introduced me and said, "My boy wants to go to college and I want to borrow the money for his tuition for his first semester." And I signed the note. My Dad co-signed. I became a borrower. That's where it started.

Now, Carolyn grew up in a family that didn't borrow money for anything. Her Daddy built their first house and paid cash as he went. When he first started, he had enough money to pour the foundation for the garage. So he did. And then he worked and worked until he had the money to buy the lumber to frame the garage. And then when he got enough money, he moved the family into the garage so he wouldn't have to borrow money to build a house. Then when he got the money, he poured the foundation for the house. But then he got the money to frame it, and he did. Next, he got enough money to finish the house and they moved in – debt free.

He paid for his cars the same way. Carolyn's Mom and Dad never had debt on anything. And they tried to teach me when she and I got married. But no. It was going to take too long to do it that way. And you know, what I wanted, I wanted now. I didn't want to wait.

What was wrong? I didn't just have debt on me, and I wasn't just in debt. Debt was *in* me. It was the way I thought. I didn't know you could do anything else other than borrow money. I didn't know how to buy a car without debt. I didn't even know how to buy a broom without debt. Here I was, newly married, trying to support a wife and go to college. I didn't know how to do that without going into debt.

While I was in college, I was called up for active duty. I was in the National Guard. It looked as though I was going to Vietnam. But Carolyn was praying. She was pregnant with our first child, and she was praying that I wouldn't have to go. We thought my unit was going, but the governor of our state decided that he wanted our unit to train with the state police riot control. Thank God, I didn't have to go and I stayed home.

When all that was behind me, I told Carolyn, "I'm not going to school any more." I said, "I am going to buy a new colored television set, and I'm going to sit around and watch football games for about two months before I even go back to work."

And that's what I did. I went down and bought a television set for $13 a month for the rest of my life. Why? Because debt was in me. I was in debt and debt was *in* me!

Notice God said, "I am gong to drive debt out of my people like leprosy out of the lepers of old."

ONE BIG PROJECT

Now, that sounds like a big project to me. How is God going to do that? It's going to take an explosion. It's going to take a major shaking. But He's God. And I am going to go ahead and stretch my mind and stretch my thoughts and stretch my thinking and get right up there on the same level with Him.

How about you? Do you believe that God can supernaturally get you out of debt?

Now, let's be honest. You might be thinking, "Jerry, you don't understand. I want to believe that I can live in the fullness of the blessing, but I just don't know. I have so much debt and I am having a hard time believing that it can actually happen to me."

Well then let me ask you this question: Do you believe that Jesus is the Anointed One?

The Spirit of the Lord [is] upon Me, because He has anointed Me [the Anointed One, the Messiah] to preach the good news (the Gospel) to the poor; He has sent Me to announce release to the captives and recovery of sight to the blind, to send forth as delivered those who are oppressed [who are downtrodden, bruised, crushed and broken down by calamity].

– Luke 4:18, Amplified

If you believe that He is the Anointed One, then there is not a devil in hell who can keep you from experiencing what God has for you. Isn't that what Jesus told the people many times? He said things like: "If you can believe . . ." or "Be it unto thee according to thy faith . . ."

All He encouraged the people to do was to "Believe what I am telling you and if you believe what I say, then you will become the recipient of deliverance, miracles, and change in your life."

But how does faith come? Faith comes when you continually hear the Word of God. Romans 10:17 says, *So then faith cometh by hearing and hearing by the Word of God.*

Just think about how many times in Matthew, Mark, Luke, and John, Jesus said things like, "And again I say unto thee..." Why? Because faith comes when you hear and hear what God's Word says.

What does unbelief do? It prevents the Anointed One from working in your life. Jesus couldn't do anything mighty in His own home town because of their unbelief.

And he marveled because of their unbelief . . .

– Mark 6:6

But notice how Jesus dealt with their unbelief.

. . . and he went round about the villages, teaching.

– Mark 6:6

What did He do about it? He taught. Why did He teach? Because faith comes by hearing.

So, if you are having trouble believing that you could ever live in the fullness of the blessing, then let me encourage you to spend more time in the Word. Go back and read it again. Get into the Word like never before. If you hear the

Word enough, then you will come to the place where you have more faith in the Word and what God says about you than you have in your circumstances.

HE CAN AND HE WILL

And let me tell you this - I know that He can do it for you. I have seen it happen to many people. I have many testimonies that people have sent to me to prove it.

I saw a vivid example of it a few months ago. I have been on the Board of Regents of Oral Roberts University since 1981. You probably remember seeing the news that the university was in a major financial crisis.

It was in debt. Huge debt. It got to the place where we thought we were on the verge of closing the doors to one of the last real Christian universities in the world. Oral Roberts put his heart and soul into that university, and it looked as though it was finished.

We were sitting in a Regents meeting faced with the decision: What do we do next? Then the Green family from Hobby Lobby came in and made a proposal. Over a period of time, and after making some adjustments that we all agreed upon, we accepted their proposal. One day we were millions of dollars in debt and faced with the question of what we were going to do, and the next thing we know the

University is out of debt. I walked over to Oral Roberts, and I said, "Brother Roberts, it just goes to prove seed faith still works. That's your harvest, sir. That's your harvest from all these years."

Now, you can't tell me that God can't supernaturally deliver you from your debt. He can. I have seen it. I've seen it big time.

If God can do that, then surely He can get you out of your debt. I don't think there are very many people reading this book that are millions of dollars in debt, but if you are, you now have an example that God can do it. The barrier has been broken.

You know if you stop and think about it, the first time God supernaturally got His people out of debt was when the Israelites left Egypt. He told them to go to the Egyptians and get all of the silver and gold that they could possibly carry out. And they did. They carried it out, as some people would say, "by the truck loads." And then when the Egyptians tried to follow them through the Red Sea, God closed the sea up. It swallowed them up. That's supernatural debt cancellation.

I have had letters written to me from people testifying about how God supernaturally cancelled their debt. I have one letter where a lady and her husband were faced with a tremendous debt with the IRS. They owed something like $85,000 in taxes, and some way or another, they negotiated with the IRS and got them to accept $40,000. They began to sow significant seed toward that breakthrough. They later got a letter from the IRS saying that they forgave them of the debt. They sent me a copy of the letter from the IRS. When I read it, I said, "Our redemption draweth nigh."

I don't know how God can do that. That's not my job. And it's not yours either. You don't have to figure out how God can do it. All you have to do is believe that He will do it for you. He said there is a blessing explosion coming. I don't think it is a hundred years down the road. I think we're in it now.

Just imagine how much better your life will be when you are debt free. Take a moment right now and just think about that.

You have got to think bigger. You have got to stretch your thinking and stretch your faith. Come up higher. It's time to go to the next level. It's time to become the lender and not the borrower. How? By living in the fullness of the blessing.

CHAPTER 4

VALUE THE BLESSING

Have you ever wondered why Adam and Eve committed high treason against God? I mean why did they do that? Just think about it. They had everything they needed. They had everything they wanted. Why would they risk losing that?

Once again, God's first words to Adam were, "Be blessed." He pronounced His blessing on Adam, and it was something that came on him that very moment. It was on him and he had the ability to do things that would cause his lifestyle to be one without limits. But Adam lost it. Why? Because he got to the place where he no longer valued it. He didn't value the blessing of God.

If he had valued the blessing, he would have never committed high treason. If he had valued it, if he had esteemed it and if it had great importance to him, instead of partaking of the fruit that God said they were not to partake of, he would have said, "No, I am not going to do that because to do that would mean to forfeit the blessing." But he didn't. He no longer valued the blessing that was on his life.

I believe that many Christians today don't value the blessing either. The word "blessing" is a just a byword to a lot of Christians. It's just something they hear spoken about in church. They may see it in the Bible, but they don't really value it. They don't esteem it like they should.

I would hate to think about what my life would be like if God's blessing wasn't on it. I don't even want to think about that. God has brought me so far from where I came from. I know you have heard me say this many times before, but I am presently living life far better than I ever dreamed possible. Why? Because of the blessing.

I know where I came from. I know that I would be nothing without the blessing on my life. And when you know that you would be nothing and that you would have nothing without the blessing of God on your life, then you prize it. You value it.

One reason why many Christians today aren't walking in a greater level of the blessing is because they don't value it.

When I asked God to show me the primary keys for positioning ourselves to move into the fullness of the blessing, He said, "The number one key that I want you to focus on is this: You have to value it. You have to value the blessing."

YOUR BEST DAYS ARE AHEAD OF YOU, NOT BEHIND YOU

Most of the people in the Old Testament understood what the blessing meant. They understood that the blessing of God on your life guaranteed a bright future.

An example of this is a man by the name of Esau.

And Jacob said, Sell me this day thy birthright. And Esau said, Behold, I am at the point to die: and what profit shall this birthright do to me?

– Genesis 25:31-32

Esau was starving. And the birthright represented the blessing. His brother wanted that blessing. And he said, "I'll sell you this food if you promise to give me the blessing" (author's paraphrase). Esau didn't value the blessing enough and he actually sold it to his brother for a plate of food.

Now later, their father Isaac is about to die, and before he dies, he's got to pronounce the blessing on the firstborn. Esau was the firstborn but he had sold his birthright to Jacob. And you might know the rest of the story. Isaac's sight was not very good, and Jacob deceived his father into giving him Esau's blessing.

Here is what Esau said when he came back and discovered that the blessing had been pronounced on his brother.

. . . Bless me, even me also, O my father.
– Genesis 27:34

What happened? Esau suddenly realized what he had lost. He suddenly realized the value of that blessing, and now he had lost it, and he was devastated. The birthright, the blessing, finally came to a place in his mind where he realized how valuable it was and now he was going to be without it.

Understand that in Old Testament times, once the blessing was bestowed, it was irretrievable. They couldn't go back and retract it. Esau now understands what is missing in his life and how it's going to affect his future. The blessing on a person's life, as described in the Old Testament, guaranteed a bright future. It does the same for you and me today.

That's the reason you should keep saying that your best days are not behind you. They are ahead of you. Why? Because you have the blessing of God on your life.

So, let me ask you: How valuable is the blessing to you today? Is it something that you just hear preached about?

Is it just something that you have seen written about in the Bible? Is "blessing" just a word to you? Or do you truly understand that the blessing is an empowerment that comes on your life and enables you to do what you cannot do in your natural might and achieve what you cannot achieve in your own natural ability? How valuable is it to you today?

BEYOND HUMAN ABILITY

God's not going to shove anything on you that you don't value or something that you will take lightly.

Stop and think how differently your life might be right now if you didn't know that the blessing of God is on your life. Living in and walking in the blessing of God starts with placing a high value on it. Esteeming it. When you have the blessing of God on your life, it inspires you. It motivates you and causes you to believe that what men say is impossible is not impossible at all.

I can tell you from personal experience that if I didn't know that I had the blessing of God on my life, I would not have even attempted some of the things we have done over the last 39 years. I know that there is something on me that enables me to tap into a strength and a power and a knowing that is beyond my own human ability. That's the blessing of God.

The blessing to you has to become like Peter talked about concerning the promises of God. Precious. Precious promises (2 Peter 1:45). When the blessing of God is precious to you, you are not so quick to take it lightly. You are not so quick to do things that might jeopardize it.

My wife is precious to me. We have been married for 42 years. She is so precious to me that I am not interested in another woman. I don't want to lose what I've got. I would have to break covenant with God and with her. We have known each other almost all our lives. She's precious to me. My relationship with her is precious, and I am not going to do anything that would jeopardize it. And that is the way you have to feel about the blessing of God.

Let me ask you once again: How important is the blessing of God to you today?

When the blessing has great value in your life, then God says that He can trust you with more of its benefits.

CHAPTER 5

AGREE THAT THE BLESSING IS ON YOU

When Carolyn and I first came into the Word of Faith, we had a lot of debts. I had shut down my automotive business to go into the ministry. Our car was worn out and we didn't have any money. We were broke.

We heard that Kenneth Copeland was preaching in Fort Worth, Texas, and we just knew that we had to be at that meeting. It was about 200 miles from where we lived at the time. We got in our car with our two babies, believing that God would get us there, and we headed to Fort Worth. The meeting was going to last for three days. Now you have to understand, like I said before, we were broke. We didn't have money for a hotel. We didn't have money to go to a restaurant after the meetings. We made peanut butter and jelly sandwiches and crackers and cheese, and we carried them with us in our car. That was what we ate.

Our plan was to go to the morning services and then go sit in our car and eat our peanut butter and jelly sandwiches and then go to the meeting that night and after the meeting, just sleep in our car. We were going to do that for the duration of the meeting. We didn't have any money but I can tell you that we were happy. *That's how I should be...*

If somebody would have come up and said, "Bless your hearts. Poor things." I would have turned around to see who they were talking to. Why? Because I knew the Word I was being taught was about to get me out of Egypt and take me to the Promised Land. Now, at that moment in our lives, it didn't look like we were blessed, but the blessing was on us. You just couldn't see the effects of it yet. It was there, but the by-products weren't – yet!

This brings me to the next key to living in the fullness of the blessing: Agree with God that the blessing is on you.

IT *IS* ON YOU

At this very moment, it may not look like the blessing of God is on your life based on your circumstances, based on your present conditions, and based on what you are going through right now. Maybe you are experiencing a lot of lack in your life. If that is the case, you have got to agree with God that the blessing is on you.

It is on you! God has pronounced His blessing on your life. So agree with Him. Don't let other people (or your circumstances) determine what you believe. Only believe what the Word says about you. The Word says you are blessed and highly favored. The Word says that you are the head and not the tail. The Word says you are above and not beneath (Deuteronomy 28). The Word says that you are the seed of Abraham and heirs according to the promise (Galatians 3:29).

No matter what your circumstances are, you have to keep proclaiming that the blessing of God is on your life, keep decreeing it and keep agreeing with God. God doesn't lie. If He says you are blessed and highly favored, then you are. So all you need to do is agree with Him.

DON'T QUIT

Don't quit just because it looks like nothing is working. That's why Paul talked about pressing. You have got to press. You have got to outlast the devil. You have got to let him know once and for all that you are in this for the long haul. You are not *trying* something. You are going to *do* it. You are going to live in the fullness of the blessing. It is going to happen.

Today, one of my favorite things to do when I find out somebody has come to one of my meetings and doesn't have money for a hotel or for food, is get them a hotel room and feed them. Why? Because the blessing came on me.

And when the blessing comes on you, you are no longer the tail. You're the head. You are no longer beneath, you're above.

God is no respecter of persons. If he can do it for this Mississippi boy, then He can do it for you!

Don't say, "Someday, Brother Jerry." No. Say it now. Agree with God now. The blessing of God is on you, even in your present circumstances.

FAITH IS NOW

Hebrews 11:1 says, *Now faith is . . .*

I like to say it this way: Faith is now.

So, put your faith in the now. If God says that His blessing is on you, then let His Word be final authority. The more you say it, the more you decree it, then the more you will believe it. And the more you believe it, eventually, your believing will turn to knowing. And when you know that you are blessed of God, when you know it's on you and that it empowers you to do the impossible and achieve things you couldn't do in the natural, then no devil will be able to talk you out of it. When you truly know that His blessing is on your life, then nothing will ever look impossible again.

Let me tell you again, it doesn't matter how much money you owe. It doesn't matter how much money you need. It doesn't matter if you are down to your last meal; agree with God right now that His blessing is on you. Say it out of your mouth. Decree it everyday, several times a day. Constantly decree that the blessing, the fullness of the blessing is on your life, and then continually praise God for it.

Every morning when you get up, look at yourself in the mirror and say, "I am highly favored. I am extremely blessed and everywhere I go today goodness and mercy are going to follow me. Blessings are going to come on me and overtake me. I am the head and not the tail, above and not beneath. Today is my receiving day!"

It doesn't matter what your circumstances look like right now. They are subject to change because there is something on you greater than your circumstances, and it is the blessing of Almighty God! So agree with God that the blessing is on you and that you live in *the* fullness of blessing and watch your circumstances come in line with God's plan for your life.

WORDS

Why is it so important to confess with your mouth that you live in the fullness of the blessing? Why do you need to agree with God? Because what you say out of your mouth matters. God knows it and the devil knows it. That is why the devil has worked so hard to deceive us into believing that what we say doesn't matter. Just think about the phrase we use to say as kids. *Sticks and stones may break my bones but words will never hurt me.*

The truth is that words can hurt you. The Bible even says they can bring death.

Death and life are in the power of the tongue . . .
– Proverbs 18:21

If you are going to agree with God that you are living in the fullness of the blessing, then you can't agree with the devil (by speaking your circumstances) at the same time. That's called mingled seed (Leviticus 19:19).

I am not saying to pretend that negative things are not happening. I am not saying to just pretend that your light bill isn't due or that your mortgage isn't due. I am not saying to pretend that sickness and disease do not exist or that marital problems don't exist. Pretending is not faith. Faith doesn't pretend. Faith attacks. And faith is now.

Your situations do not change the Word of God. What will change your situation is when you get your words in line with THE Word, and THE Word says that you are blessed and highly favored.

. . . let no corrupt communication proceed out of your mouth . . .

– Ephesians 4:29

Most people think that verse is talking about "cussing." And it definitely includes cussing or profanity. But as far as God is concerned, there is more to corrupt communication than just cussing.

God can't come in agreement with you if all you talk about is poverty, lack, sickness, disease, failure, and defeat. That is not what He talks about. Now, if you ask Him what He has to say about that, He will say, "I have redeemed you, and I said, Let the redeemed of the Lord say so. Talk about your redemption. Let's talk about that."

BE FREE

Instead of speaking words that keep you bound, learn to speak words that set you free. When Paul said that we should not let any corrupt communication proceed from our mouth (Ephesians 4:29), he was talking about words that destroy, words that ruin, words that bring decay into our lives. Don't speak words that are going to make your situation worse. Speak words that will bring life and freedom.

For by thy words thou shalt be justified, and by thy words thou shalt be condemned.

— Matthew 12:37

Justified means to be deemed right. In other words, when you line up your words with God's Word, then He will honor your obedience and you will be blessed.

Condemned means you have pronounced a verdict on yourself. When you are talking things contrary to God's Word then you have pronounced your own sentence. Solomon said it this way:

Thou art snared with the words of thy mouth, thou art taken with the words of thy mouth.

— Proverbs 6:2

The word *snared* means trapped. When you are talking contrary to the Word of God then you are setting a trap for yourself. One of the Greek words that has been translated into the English word "snare" is noose. Like a hangman's noose. In other words, you can hang yourself with your words.

A good man out of the good treasure of the heart bringeth forth good things: and an evil man out of the evil treasure bringeth forth evil things.

— Matthew 12:35

Your words are going to come to pass. Your tongue holds the power of life and death in it. You have to choose which it will be. Will it be life or will it be death? Will it be living in the fullness of the blessing or will it be continuing on the same path?

You can't live in the fullness of the blessing the way God wants you to if you are constantly speaking words that are contrary to His Word.

The Bible tells us that Jesus, according to Hebrews 3:1, is *"the Apostle and High Priest of our profession . . . ."* W.E. Vines translates this word profession into the word confession. Jesus is the Apostle and High Priest of our confession. When we are speaking God's words then Jesus can get in agreement with us and watch over them to perform them. He cannot be the high priest of your words, or your confession, if they don't line up with God's Word. He can only come into agreement with you when you choose to speak His Words.

WORDS IN MOTION

When you speak God's Word, it also releases the angels to work in your behalf. Speaking about angels, the author of the book of Hebrews wrote in Hebrews 1:14 - *Are they not all ministering spirits sent forth to minister for them who shall be heirs of salvation?* The author of Hebrews is telling us that the angels are sent forth to minister for you and me. We are the heirs of salvation. When you made Jesus the Lord of your life then you became an heir of salvation. Now the angels work for you, but you have to give them something to work with.

Psalm 103:20 says, *Bless the Lord, ye his angels, that excel in strength, that do his commandments, hearkening unto the voice of his word.* Notice what the angels have been commanded by God to do: hearken to His Word. They are to listen for His Word. And once they hear His Word, they are to cause it to come to pass.

How do they hear God's Word? They hear it one of three ways:
1)   When God speaks it
2)   When Jesus speaks it
3)   When you and I speak it

When you are speaking the Word, all of the angels stand at attention. They recognize the language you are speaking. They say, "He is talking our language. He is speaking the Word." What does the Bible say they do when they hear His Word? They excel in strength, hearkening unto the voice of God's Word to do it.

When you are speaking the Word over your circumstances, over your feelings, over your symptoms, then you have gotten the attention of the angels. Their job is to go make the Word come to pass! They only hearken to God's Word. They don't hearken to doubt and unbelief. They don't hearken to words that are contrary to God's Word. It is only when we speak God's Word that we can expect the angels to move in our behalf. When they hear the Word out of your mouth, they begin to busy themselves in endeavoring to bring the Word to pass in your life.

CHAPTER 6

KEEP YOUR LIFE PURE

At Jerry Savelle Ministries, at the beginning of every new year, we have a staff meeting. This is when I share with my staff what I believe God wants us to do for that year, our vision, our goals, and so forth. The last thing my staff hears every year is that I pledge and I promise to them that I will keep my life pure, that I will not disappoint them by being a bad example and a bad representative of Jesus Christ. I do that not just for them but also out of gratitude to God for the blessing that is on my life.

And the same should be true for you. If you are deeply grateful for this blessing that God has given you, then you will show it by keeping your life pure.

Another key to living in the fullness of the blessing of God is this: Show God how much you appreciate the blessing by keeping your life pure.

You might be thinking, "Wait a minute, Jerry, what about saying thank you?"

Well, saying thank you to God is wonderful, and you should thank God for the blessing, but I believe the greatest expression of your thankfulness of the blessing is keeping your life pure.

This is what Paul was talking about in Colossians 1:10:

That you may walk (live and conduct yourselves) in a manner worthy of the Lord, fully pleasing to Him and desiring to please Him in all things . . . (Amplified).

So once again, the greatest expression of your gratitude for God placing this blessing on your life is through keeping your life pure.

One of the greatest examples of this in the Bible is that of a man named Joseph. The blessing of God was on this man's life. It was on his life in such a powerful way that it showed up everywhere he went no matter what his circumstances were.

His brothers sold him into slavery, and he eventually became the property of Potipher, an Egyptian captain. But even as a slave, the Bible says in Genesis 39:2, *and the Lord was with Joseph.* That's just another way of saying the blessing was upon his life. Even as a slave, the blessing was upon Joseph.

If you read the story, it doesn't matter where you put this guy, the blessing would show up. If you put him in good and favorable circumstances, the blessing would show up or if you put him in slavery and in prison, the blessing would still show up. The blessing would manifest everywhere he went. If you read Genesis 39, it says that God prospered Joseph. He was a prosperous man.

IT'S NOT LUCK – IT'S THE BLESSING

It's one thing when you know the blessing of God is on your life, but it's something else when other people know it. They may not be able to tell you exactly what it is, but they know there is something on you that makes you different from most people.

I can't tell you the number of times over the last 39 years that I have had people say to me, "You're the luckiest guy I have ever met. I've never seen a guy with more luck than you." It's not luck. I don't operate in luck. Luck has nothing to do with my life. It's the blessing. And God is no respecter of persons. He doesn't love me (or Joseph) any more than He loves you. He loves you just as much. He wants people to notice that there is something different about you too.

The blessing made Joseph a prosperous man, and even Potipher noticed it. The Bible says in Genesis 39:3, *And his master* (speaking of Potipher) *saw that the Lord was with*

him and that the Lord made all that he did to prosper . . .
Not only did the blessing cause Joseph to prosper, but the
Bible also says, *And Joseph . . . was well favoured.* (Genesis 39:6)

Joseph was so appreciative of the blessing that was on
his life that when Potipher's wife tried to seduce him, he
would not yield. Why? Because he knew that it would not
be pleasing to God.

*. . . how then can I do this great wickedness, and sin
against God?*

– Genesis 39:9

What is he saying? Joseph was saying that he was appreciative of the blessing of God that was on his life and he
was going to show God how appreciative he was by keeping his life pure.

This is a vital key to living in the fullness of the blessing.
We don't hear a lot of teaching on this, particularly in our
faith circles. We want to sweep some things under the rug
sometimes. But how you conduct your life has everything
to do with how much of the fullness of the blessing you
will walk in.

Even though Potipher's wife lied to her husband about
Joseph and it caused Joseph to be thrown into prison, he

would not compromise his stand. He made up his mind that it didn't matter what they did to him or where they put him. He knew there was something that God had put on his life that would cause him to be prosperous whatever they did with him.

Joseph knew that if they put him in the lowest pit, it didn't matter because God would bless him in that pit. And that's exactly what God did. Why? Because he showed God how appreciative he was of the blessing that was on his life by keeping his life pure.

. . . The Lord was with him, and that which he did, the Lord made it to prosper.

— Genesis 39:23

Eventually Joseph, a slave, thrown into prison for something he did not do, became the Prime Minister of Egypt. God promoted him. God exalted him. Why? Because he was appreciative of the blessing that was on his life, and he showed it by keeping his life pure.

NO COMPROMISE

The Apostle Paul tells us in Philippians 2:15 that you and I live in a crooked and perverse world. The world we live in today has gone absolutely nuts. Who would have ever dreamed 30 years ago of the kind of sin that is just blatant and right out in front in America today? Sodom and Gomorrah had nothing on today's society. You can be just as perverse, perverted as you want to be and the government will probably give you the right to be that way.

Isaiah saw this in the spirit and prophesied that when the world is full of darkness and the minds of men are in total darkness that is when the glory of the Lord is going to be seen upon us.

As the world gets darker and darker, then the church will get brighter and brighter. But that means that you and I have a responsibility. We live in a perverse and crooked world. We live in a world that is constantly trying to get us to compromise our stand. Satan wants you to yield to this perversion so that he can prevent you from walking in the fullness of the blessing.

BE HOLY

Are you living a godly lifestyle or have you accepted the world's standards for moral conduct?

. . . and ye shall be holy; for I am holy . . .
– Leviticus 11:44

Many people don't like that verse. It's not in their confession packet. Why not? Because "be ye" requires something. It speaks of responsibility. So you have to ask yourself: What about my lifestyle?

Have you noticed how hard it is to find a television program that is not promoting the world's low standard of moral conduct? I don't use foul language. I don't cuss, but it is becoming more and more difficult to find a television broadcast that doesn't have foul language in it. I mean there are words that used to never be spoken in public, and you sure didn't speak them at all if you were a Christian, and now they have just become everyday, acceptable language. The same thing with using the Lord's name in vain. How many times have you heard "Jesus Christ" said in vain? That grieves the Holy Spirit.

Teaching us that, denying ungodliness and worldly lusts, we should live soberly, righteously, and godly, in this present world.

– Titus 2: 12

Abstain from evil [Shrink from it and keep aloof from it] in whatever form or whatever kind it may be.

– I Thessalonians 5:22 (Amplified)

Our disregard for God's standards for moral behavior has everything to do with not experiencing the fullness of the blessing like God intended. You simply cannot compromise God's standards and expect to live in the fullness of the blessing.

DON'T MISS THE MARK

The word "sin" in the Greek literally means *to miss the mark*. It is also described as falling short.

I don't want to fall short of God's best. How about you?

Look at it like this. What if you lived your whole life just barely getting by, living from paycheck to paycheck and just about the time you were about to die, you found out that you had a rich uncle that had left you an inheritance and you didn't know about it until the day you were dying. Wouldn't that make you a little perturbed? To know that your whole life you had been living paycheck to paycheck only to find out that an inheritance was waiting for you all along and you didn't know about it.

That's what sin does. It causes you to miss the mark. It causes you to fall short. That's what Paul was talking about in Romans 3:23, *All have sinned and fallen short of the glory of God*. What's the glory of God? The manifested presence of God. I don't want to fall short of that. I want God's best.

My attitude is that I have traveled too many miles, preached too many sermons, slept in too many hotels, flown on too many airlines, stayed in too many other countries, and prayed too many prayers to blow it all now. Not me. I am not going to do that.

Sometimes I go to meetings and get started talking about things like this, and they say I am old fashioned. Well, if that's what you want to call it, then fine. But the blessing is increasing in my life. Why? Because I keep my life pure. And if you don't keep your life pure, then you limit how much of God's best you can enjoy.

DEAL WITH IT

Now, if you've blown it, if you've missed the mark, if you've fallen short, then confess it to Him. We have an advocate with the Father, even the righteous Jesus Christ. He says that if we confess our sin, He is faithful and just to forgive us and give us a fresh start. Not only that, He said He will remember our iniquities no more.

So if you've been involved in something that was a mistake, don't condemn yourself. But don't just sweep it under the rug either. Deal with it. Deal with it scripturally. Ask God to forgive you, and then work on correcting it and don't be so easily tempted the next time. That's what resisting the devil is all about.

The Bible tells us to resist the devil and he will flee from you. You have to resist every opportunity that he presents to you that is designed to get you to compromise.

When I first went into the ministry, I was amazed at the opportunities that came to compromise. I remember my first trip with Kenneth Copeland. A woman called me and propositioned me. She began to describe in detail what she was willing to do. I slammed the phone down. It scared me. I started praying in tongues. I didn't know people talked to preachers like she talked to me. I thought, "Dear God, some crazy woman's lusting after me out there."

And she didn't stop. She kept calling me. She would call me all day. She would call me into the night. I remember thinking that I couldn't tell Kenneth Copeland because I thought he would cast the devils out of me and then fire me. I was shook up over this whole deal. I didn't know what to do.

Then one day, I told him what happened. I told him exactly what this woman had said. He started laughing.

Now, I didn't see the humor in this at all. I said, "What are you laughing at?"

He reached out and shook my hand and said, "Welcome to the ministry. Now you know you're a precious life, and now you know you're a threat to the devil, and now you know that the anointing of God is on you to and Satan is trying to trip you up before you can even get started good."

Well, it's been almost 40 years now and I am still here and I am living in the blessing more than ever before. Why? Because I think too highly of the blessing to do anything to jeopardize it. I think too highly of what God has done in my life through the blessing. And I'm going to demonstrate my attitude not just by saying "thank you" every once in a while but by living my life pure everyday.

Once again, I know this is not a topic that is discussed very much. But it is vital. If you want to live in the fullness of the blessing, then show God how appreciative and how grateful you are for the blessing by keeping your life pure.

CHAPTER 7

LOOK FOR EVERY OPPORTUNITY TO GIVE

To acquire something you want, then you must be willing to sow something you already have.

I was in a city one time preaching for a Pastor friend of mine. It was a Sunday morning service, and so after the service was over, he took me to a cafeteria to eat. We went down the line getting our food, and then we came to the person at the register who adds up your bill. The man commented on the tie that I was wearing.

He said, "Mister, that is the most beautiful tie I've ever seen."

I said, "Well, thank you."

He said, "I've never seen a tie like that. Did you buy that here in town?"

I told him that I was just visiting and that I hadn't bought the tie in his town. I told him that I had bought it in London while preaching there.

He said, "I wish my wife was here. My birthday's coming up and if I could find a tie like that I'd tell her that's what I want for my birthday."

Well, I reached up, untied it, and gave it to him. I said, "You really like this tie?"

He said, "I do."

I said, "Well, here. I'd like to bless you with it."

"Oh no. I couldn't do that. I didn't mean that I wanted you to give it to me."

"No. No. No. I want you to understand you are an answer to my prayer."

He said, "What?"

I said, "You are an answer to my prayer. I got up this morning, and I said, 'Lord, give me an opportunity to sow some seed. Bring me an opportunity to sow some seed.' You're an answer to my prayer. I have been looking all day for an opportunity to sow and you're the answer to my prayer. Here. Receive it."

I believe we should look for opportunities to sow every day!

A rich young ruler came to Jesus one time and he wanted something. He wanted to acquire something. "How may I inherit eternal life?" (author's paraphrase). He wanted something that he didn't have (Matthew 19:16).

Jesus said, "Go and sell what you have and give." Matthew 19:21 (author's paraphrase)

Notice, to acquire something that you want, you have to first of all be willing to sow something you already have.

LOOK FOR THE OPPORTUNITIES

This is another key the Lord shared with me about positioning ourselves for walking in the fullness of the blessing: Look for every opportunity that you can to sow towards the fulfillment of this.

Carolyn and I learned years ago that when we see something in the Word that we believe is about to take us to another level, the first thing we do is sow a seed in faith toward the fulfillment of that.

You can't have a harvest without sowing. Harvests just don't happen. They are the results of sowing. And if you want manifestations of the fullness of the blessing in your life, then you should sow toward that.

I asked the Lord to show me an example of this, and of course, the first thing He said to me was this, "The entire earth revolves around this principle."

While the earth remains, seedtime and harvest, shall not cease.

– Genesis 8:22 (Amplified)

The whole earth revolves around the principle of sowing and reaping. The world calls it cause and effect. For every action, there is a reaction.

Then, He took me to Genesis 12.

In Genesis 12, God told Abraham that He would bless him. God said, "I will bless you. I will make you a blessing. I will make your name great. I will make a nation out of you and that through you all the families of the earth will be blessed."

This is what God promised Abraham when He first introduced Himself to him. He was known as Abram at that time. God also told him that if he would arise and walk through the land, that He would give him the length of it and the breadth of it. He told him that He would give him a son and that this son would come from his wife, Sarah. Now, at this time, it was impossible for Sarah to conceive, but God told him, "She will bare you a son and from this son, your seed will be as many as the stars in the heaven and the pebbles of sand on the seashore."

But did Abraham wait until all of those promises were manifested before he started sowing? No. He did not.

God is talking about these promises in Genesis 12, 13, and 14. By chapter 15, for the first time mentioned in the Bible, it says that Abraham gave Melchizedek tithes of all. Once again, the promises that God gave Abraham haven't been fulfilled yet.

What was Abraham doing?

He was not only giving God tithes of all, showing his appreciation for God being his source and showing appreciation for the blessing that was on his life, but he is sowing towards the fulfillment of the promises that God had given him.

Over the years, I have learned to follow that example. And if you want to live in the fullness of the blessing, then let me encourage you to begin to look for every opportunity that you can to sow towards the fulfillment of it. If you do, then you won't be disappointed. I can tell you without any reservations that God has never let me down.

Abraham was sowing out of his love for God. He was sowing out of his respect for God. But, he was also sowing towards the fulfillment of those promises.

Let me encourage you to do the same thing. Sow toward the fulfillment of living in the fullness of the blessing. And don't just sow every once in a while but do it every opportunity you can find.

The Bible says in Galatians 6 that we are to look for opportunities to be a blessing, to be a sower, and to get some seed into someone else's life.

IT'S NOT SUBTRACTION, IT'S ADDITION

I have found that a lot of people look at giving to God as God taking something away from them. That's not true. Even though what you give may leave your hand, it never leaves your life.

When you sow your tithes and offerings on Sunday your attitude shouldn't be: "Bye. Nice to have had you for a while." No. What you gave did leave your hand, but it didn't leave your life. God never forgets a seed sown. You are sowing towards your future. You are sowing towards the fulfillment of the promises that God has said are yours.

When you wake up in the morning, your attitude should be, "I live to give." Remember the law of seedtime and harvest is the principle that the whole earth revolves around.

Always give in joy. If you don't give in joy, then you aren't doing it in faith either.

. . . God loveth a cheerful giver . . .

– 2 Corinthians 9:7

"Well, the Lord's making me give this up." If that is your attitude, then that's not giving in joy. That's not giving in faith. You should be joyful in your giving. Why? Because you are making an investment in your future. You can't out give God. The more you sow, then the greater the measure of the fullness of the blessing that you will walk in.

CHAPTER 8

BLESSING BLOCKERS

By now you understand that God wants you living in the fullness of the blessing. No matter what level of that blessing you are walking in now, He wants you experiencing more in your life. We have spent the last several chapters talking about what you need to do to get into position for experiencing the fullness of the blessing. Now I want to talk to you about some things that can block you from living in it.

I like to call them blessing blockers. If we can discover the things in our lives that are keeping us from experiencing the fullness of the blessing, then we can remove them. We can correct it so that we can get on with enjoying God's best.

As the bird by wandering, and as the swallow by flying, so the curse causeless shall not come.

– Proverbs 26:2

. . . the curse causeless shall not come. In other words, curses do not have a right to operate in your life without a cause.

I want to refer to the "curse" as a blocked blessing. That is what a curse is. It is something that is keeping you from experiencing the blessing of God in your life.

So, a curse or a blessing blocker has to have some kind of foundation. It has to have some kind of reason or explanation. There has to be a cause for it or it can't take place.

DISOBEDIENCE

And it shall come to pass, if thou shalt hearken diligently unto the voice of the Lord thy God, to observe and to do all his commandments which I command thee this day, that the Lord thy God will set thee on high above all nations of the earth: And all these blessings shall come on thee and overtake thee . . .

– Deuteronomy 28:1-2

If you continue to read on, it becomes obvious that God wants to bless us in every area of our lives. He wants to bless us financially, physically, mentally, and socially. But, there is a condition – if you will hearken diligently unto the voice of the Lord thy God and obey.

Obedience brings living in the fullness of the blessing. Disobedience gives the curse a cause.

But it shall come to pass, if thou wilt not hearken unto the voice of the Lord thy God, to observe to do all his commandments and his statutes which I command thee this day; that all these curses shall come upon thee, and overtake thee.

— Deuteronomy 28:15

Obedience opens the door to the blessings, and disobedience blocks the blessings.

Jesus tells us the same thing in John 10:27. He says, *My sheep hear my voice . . . and they follow me.* Jesus is saying that His people hear His voice and they follow Him. To follow would mean they obey Him.

Another example would be Mary, the mother of Jesus. She said it this way, *Whatsoever he saith unto you, do it.* (John 2:5).

The basic requirement for being blessed is still the same today as it was under the old covenant – obedience. Disobedience is a major problem in the body of Christ today.

Jesus once asked His disciples in Luke 6:46 (Amplified), *Why do you call Me, Lord, Lord and do not [practice] what I tell you?* Why do you keep saying that I am your Lord, but you don't do what I tell you? (author's paraphrase)

How many times do you suppose that you have ignored God's instructions? You know what I am talking about. God tells you to do something and you decide that you will do it later or not at all. How many times has God spoken to you about giving to someone and you hesitated or you fussed with it or you came up with a better idea or you sent a lower figure?

How many times do you suppose we disobey and don't even think twice about it? Jesus said that His sheep hear His voice and they follow Him. In other words, they are obedient. They do what He tells them to do.

In the book of James, we see that obedience is a vital key for the blessings of God to flow your way. James 1:22, *But be ye doers of the word, and not hearers only . . . .* Then, he said if you are a hearer only, then you are deceiving yourself.

But in James 1:25, he says, that the doer will be blessed in his deeds. So notice that obedience is just as important in the New Testament as it was in the Old Testament.

The psalmist tells us that if we are doers of the Word, then we will prosper in whatsoever we do (Psalm 1:3). On the other hand, Moses tells us in Deuteronomy 28 that disobedience will block our blessings. Disobedience will block God's best for our lives.

And thou shalt grope at noonday, as the blind gropeth in darkness, and thou shalt not prosper in all thy ways: and thou shalt be only oppressed and spoiled evermore . . .

— Deuteronomy 28:29

"Spoiled evermore" would mean that you just gave the devil a right to steal everything you have. He is a thief and he will steal everything you have when you open the door through disobedience.

Therefore thou shalt serve thine enemies which the Lord shall send against thee, in hunger, and in thirst, and in nakedness, and in want of all things . . .

— Deuteronomy 28:48

Notice that Moses was also telling us that disobedience opens the door to continual financial lack. If there is continual financial lack in your life, then I would suggest searching your heart and asking yourself where you have been disobedient.

Someone once told me, "When it seems like nothing is working and it seems like your mountains are not moving but they appear to be getting bigger, check up on yourself and make sure you did the last thing God told you to do."

I like to write down what the Lord tells me to do so that I can go back and use it as a checklist. If you will write a list, then you can use it to make sure that you have done everything God told you to do.

TAKE RESPONSIBILITY

We have to take full responsibility for ourselves. Don't be looking everywhere else. Where have I been disobedient?

If "in want of all things" describes your life today, this can be corrected. It is not a permanent situation. Search your heart. Ask the Holy Spirit to reveal to you where you have missed it. Where you have been disobedient?

THE BIG THREE

Let's take a look at three different areas where you might have been disobedient or where maybe you have failed to be a doer of the Word.

#1. Ask yourself if you are putting God first place in your life or have you let things become more important to you. *But seek ye first the kingdom of God, and his righteousness, and all these things shall be added unto you.*

— Matthew 6:33

We live in a world where we need a lot of things. We need the material necessities of life like food, clothing, and shelter. But most of the time food, clothing, and shelter are not enough. We want other things. God is not against you having things but He is against things having you.

We are told in the Scripture to "love God with all our hearts, all our might, and all our strength." Are you obeying this command? If you are, then Satan does not have the right to block your blessings. If you can truly say that your primary pursuit in life is God and not things, then that door has been shut and Satan cannot use that avenue to block your blessings.

#2. Are you walking in love or is there strife and unforgiveness in your heart?

A new commandment I give unto you, That ye love one another; as I have loved you, that ye also love one another.
$\qquad$ – John 13:34

Jesus said we are to love one another. Are you doing that? We cannot walk in the fullness of the blessing when we refuse to walk in love. No matter how difficult it might seem, forgive. Stay out of strife. Get rid of bitterness. It is a blessing blocker.

#3. Are you honoring God with your tithes and your offerings or are you robbing Him?

In Zechariah 5:3, God declares that a curse comes on the house of a person who is a thief. Now, you might be thinking, "I am not a thief, Jerry. He is just talking about people who rob from other people." No. He just said a thief.

Will a man rob God? Yet ye have robbed me. But ye say, Wherein have we robbed thee? In tithes and offerings. Ye are cursed with a curse . . .

– Malachi 3:8-9

In other words, because you don't honor God with your tithes and offerings, living in the fullness of the blessing has been blocked. God calls the tithes holy, and He also says, "It is Mine." He lays claim to it. So if you are using it for other things, then you are being disobedient.

The proper attitude for tithing is to set it aside first. Don't pay everybody else and then if there is anything left over bring it to God. That is not being a doer of the Word, and that kind of attitude will block your blessings.

. . . let every one of you lay by him in store, as God hath prospered him . . .

– 1 Corinthians 16:2

Put aside something and save it up as he has prospered...

– 1 Corinthians 16:2 (Amplified)

Maybe you need to get a special checking account and call it your "tithing account" or "giving account." Get it out of your everyday usage so that you are not tempted to use it for something else. Get the tithe out of your general account. It does not belong to you.

If you don't begin to discipline yourself to take the tithe out first, then you will always struggle with this. Tithing is something you must be consistent about. If you only tithe when it's convenient, it will not bring the fullness of the blessing in your life.

I can promise you that your money will go a lot farther on 90% and giving God his 10% than it will when you keep 100%. So, giving to God consistently has got to become part of your lifestyle. It should be first nature to you.

WIPE THE SLATE CLEAN

When your blessing seems to be blocked, then go through this checklist. Be honest with yourself and then make whatever corrections you need to make.

Ask God to forgive you. Say what David said in Psalm 67:1, *God be merciful unto us.* And then he said, . . . *and bless us.*

In other words, "God I am asking You to wipe the slate clean and then bless me. God, thank you for forgiving me. I am sorry for being disobedient. I stand corrected, and now let Your blessings flow once again in my life."

...And God, even our God, shall bless us.

– Psalm 67:6

When you can ask for forgiveness, God will forgive you, and the barriers will be removed. The cause for the curse will be removed and the blessings will flow.

CHAPTER 9

CATCH THE VISION

The most pathetic person in the world is someone who has sight but has no vision. – Helen Keller

Let me ask you today: What do you see when you look at yourself in the mirror? Do you see somebody living in the fullness of the blessing or do you see somebody who is struggling just to get by. Do you see yourself always coming up short and always in debt or do you see somebody who is living in the fullness of the blessing like God has planned for them?

What is your vision today?

. . . And the Lord said unto Abram after that Lot was separated, lift up now thine eyes and look from the place where thou art northward and southward and eastward and westward. For all the land which thou seeth to thee will I giveth and to thy seed for ever. And I will make thy seed as the dust of the earth: So if a man can number the dust of the earth then shall thy seed also be numbered. Arise,

and walk through the land and the length of it and in the breadth of it; for I will give it.

— Genesis 13:14-17 (ASV)

Notice the phrase *lift up thine eyes and look.* What was God doing? What was He telling Abraham?

God is saying to him, "I want you to look at something, and if you will look at what I am telling you to look at, it's going to create a permanent vision on the inside of you for what I want you to have" (author's paraphrase). God is endeavoring to teach Abraham how to develop a vision. God wants Abraham to catch the vision of increase. He wants him to catch the vision of living in the fullness of the blessing that God had in store for him.

God wants Abraham to get to the point where when he looks at himself, he no longer sees one man but he sees a nation. Every time Abraham looks at the sand, God wants him to not just see sand but see descendants. At one point, He even told him to go out and look at all the stars and that if he could count the number of stars in the sky, then that's how many his seed would be.

What was God endeavoring to do? Create a vision on the inside of Abraham. God wants Abraham to catch the vision that He has for his life. And He wants you to do the same thing. He wants you to catch the vision He has for your life.

And what is God's vision for your life? Living in the fullness of the blessing. He wants you increasing in every area of your life. That's His vision for you. Increase.

IT ALL BEGINS WITH A VISION

When Carolyn and I first started learning about this, we didn't have any monetary seed to sow. Like I have said earlier, we were broke. But God changed all of that. Right now our biggest household "expense" is our giving. Why did it change? Because we began to get a vision of increase. We began to understand our covenant rights, and we began to understand that the blessing was on us. Once we saw in the Word that living in the fullness of the blessing was our covenant right, then we began developing a vision for it.

One of the verses that really helped me in those early days was: *Now he that ministereth seed to the sower both minister bread for your food, and multiply your own seed . . .* (2 Corinthians 9:10).

It was the Amplified Version of that verse that really helped perfect my vision. It says, *And [God] Who provides seed for the sower and bread for eating will also provide and multiply your resources for sowing...*

Notice that last phrase. *He will provide and multiply you're resources for sowing.* Let's just say for instance that you are a tither. That means you are giving 10% of your income, but then you are also a giver of offerings over and above your tithe. So, let's say that you give another 10% in offerings. Now you are giving 20% of your income into tithes and into offerings. Notice that it says that He will multiply your resources for sowing. If He is multiplying your resources for sowing, then He is also multiplying your resources for living. Right?

If you have more to sow that means you also have more to live on. So that helped perfect God's vision for my life over 39 years ago. When I saw that God promised that He would multiply my resources for sowing. I started saying by faith, when I had very little to sow, that God was multiplying my resources for sowing. That is exactly what He has done over the years. He has multiplied my resources for sowing.

The principle here is that you cannot out give God. You will never be able to out give Him, no matter how much you give. Once again, if you are able to sow more, then obviously you are in a position to receive more. Right?

What did God tell Abraham? Look and see, look and see. Let me ask you again: What do you see today? Do you see increase coming your way? Do you see financial breakthroughs coming your way? Do you see yourself getting out of debt? Do you see yourself being able to pay cash for your next automobile? Do you see yourself, perhaps for the first time in your life, paying the mortgage off and it not taking thirty years? Can you see that?

Lift up thine eyes and see. Catching God's vision for your life is what it takes in order for living in the fullness of the blessing to become a reality in your life. You have to be able to see yourself living that way on the inside in order for it to become a reality in your life.

PERFECTED VISION

It all begins with a vision, and the only way that that vision can come and be developed and perfected is quality time in the Word. In 2 Corinthians 3:18 it says, *But we, all with open face beholding as in a glass the glory of the Lord, are changed into the same image from glory, to glory even as by the spirit of the Lord.* The Amplified says it this way, *And all of us, as with unveiled face, [because we] continue to behold [in the word of God] as in a mirror . . .*

Notice that the Word of God is compared to a mirror. And God says as you continue to look in the mirror of His Word, you are constantly being transfigured and changed into His very own image and ever-increasing splendor and from one degree of glory to another. The more time you spend in the Word of God, then the more you are going to be changed into the image of Jesus.

You could say it this way: The more you look into God's Word as a mirror, then you will see a clearer image of yourself in God's eyes. Why? Because the Word doesn't reveal what you look like in the world's eyes, it is the way you look to God.

That's the reason you can't find in the Word where God sees you sick or broke and barely getting by. No. God sees you as an overcomer and more than a conqueror. God sees you living in the fullness of the blessing He has pronounced on your life. The more you look into the Word of God, then the more you are going to see yourself the way God sees you, and you will catch His vision for your life. God wants you to see yourself the way He sees you. How do you do that? By spending time in the Word.

DON'T PERISH

Where there is no vision, the people perish . . .

– Proverbs 29:18

If people can't see what God is doing, then they stumble . . . But when they attend to what he reveals, they are most blessed.

– Proverbs 29:18 (Message translation)

If you don't have God's vision in your heart, then when you die, you will have never taped into God's best for your life. If you can't see on the inside what God wants for you, then it will never manifest on the outside. My challenge to you is to lift up your eyes and look. Look beyond your circumstances. Stop looking at what you can see in the natural. Start looking through the eye of faith and start seeing yourself living in the fullness of the blessing.

When you get to the place that you can see what God sees, then you will be "most blessed." That sounds to me like living in the fullness of the blessing. How about you?

WHAT VISION WILL DO IN YOUR LIFE

I have found four things over the last 39 years that vision will do in your life.

1) Vision will enable you to see life the way God wants you to live it.
2) Vision will ignite your desire for the kind of life that God wants you to live.
3) Vision will enable you to stay focused on God's plan for your life.
4) Vision produces the perseverance that you will need while you are waiting for your vision to come to pass.

VISION ENABLES YOU TO SEE THE LIFE THE WAY GOD WANTS YOU TO LIVE IT

As I have already said, you have to be able to see yourself living in the fullness of the blessing in your heart before you will ever see it happening on the outside. I didn't start prospering until after I saw myself prosperous and that was when I had nothing in the natural.

When I got into the Word and found out God wanted me to prosper (*But I wish above all things that thou mayest prosper and be in health, even as thy soul prospereth.* 3 John 2) I began to see myself prosperous. Even though I still had debts and even though I still had bills up to my eyeballs, even when it looked like there was no way I could pay everything off, something had changed on the inside of me. I saw what God saw. God saw me as prosperous and so did I. That's what vision is. It is the ability to see what God sees.

The dictionary defines vision as a mental image. It is the ability to see something that has not yet manifested in the natural realm.

By faith, Abraham, when he was called to go out into a place which he should after receive for an inheritance, obeyed, and he went out, not knowing wither he went. By faith he sojourned in the land of promise, as in a strange

country, dwelling in tabernacles with Isaac and Jacob, the heirs with him of the same promise: For he looked for a city which hath foundations, whose builder and maker is God.
                                                        – Hebrews 11:8-10

What was driving Abraham? He was looking for something that he could not see in the natural realm.

By an act of faith, Abraham said yes to God's call to travel to an unknown place that would become his home. When he left, he had no idea where he was going. By an act of faith he lived in the country promised him, lived as a stranger camping in tents. Isaac and Jacob did the same . . . living under the same promise. Abraham did it by keeping an eye on an unseen city. Message translation

Abraham did it by keeping his eyes on an unseen city. Why was Abraham was able to do this? Because he had a vision. What God had said to him created a vision on the inside of him. Notice that something was "driving him" so to speak. It was his vision. He saw something that other people couldn't see and it got him up in the morning. It put him to bed at night. And even though he spent some time living in tents, he didn't get discouraged.

Sometimes you have to live in a tent before you get to the palace; but don't get discouraged while you are in the tent. Keep your eyes on the palace. Don't get discouraged while you are driving that old worn out car. Keep your eyes on what's coming. Keep your eyes on living in the fullness of the blessing.

Abraham saw what God saw and it motivated him. It kept him moving forward. It would not allow him to give up when it looked as though it would never come to pass. Once again, Abraham saw what God saw. That's what vision is - the ability to see what God sees. If you can't see what God sees, then you will never have all that God wants you to have.

Allow what God sees to become what you see. Allow His vision for your life to become your vision for your life. If you continue to see yourself as always living from paycheck to paycheck, then that is what is going to happen. If you continue to see yourself barely getting by, then that is how you will always live your life. But, if you will see yourself living in the fullness of the blessing, then that's what will happen, and eventually, you will get there.

VISION IGNITES YOUR DESIRE FOR THE KIND OF LIFE GOD WANTS YOU TO LIVE

The dictionary defines *desire* as *something longed for or something craved for.* Everybody understands desire. The word *crave* is defined as *intense desire.*

That means you are no longer wishing. You don't get anything by wishing for it. Jesus said, *What things soever ye desire . . .* Mark 11:24. He didn't say, "Whatsoever things ye wish for." Wishing has nothing to do with what we are talking about. We are talking about desire.

The word *intense* means *expressing strong emotion and being firmly fixed on having something.*

Having vision also ignites intense desire for your vision. But, if you don't truly desire your vision, you won't pursue it. The things that you currently possess in your life right now more than likely started with a desire. If you are living in your dream house, you had to desire it first. Right? If you are married to that man or woman of your dreams, you had to desire him or her first. Do you understand what I am saying?

If you desire something intensely, you will go after it with everything you have got. You will go after it with all your heart.

If living in the fullness of the blessing is not a vision yet, then your desire, which is a spiritual force, will not be ignited. Your vision ignites your desire. It will set it on fire. You will begin to desire it so much that you are determined to have it. You will become firmly fixed on living your vision. You will become intense about it and refuse to give up until it manifests in your life.

This is what Paul was referring to when he said in Philippians 3:14, *I press toward the mark* . . . The Message translation says . . . *I'm off and running and I'm not turning back.*

Once again, vision ignites your desire to have all that God says is rightfully yours. So make it your intense desire to live in the fullness of the blessing. Become firmly fixed on seeing it come to pass and refuse to give up. If you won't give up, you will eventually get there.

VISION ENABLES YOU TO STAY FOCUSED ON GOD'S PLAN FOR YOUR LIFE

When you have a vision on the inside of you, it is going to help you stay focused.

But why is it so necessary that you stay focused? Why doesn't God just do this stuff and make it so that we don't have to do anything. Well, that might be nice if it happened that way, but if it did, it would never develop the character of Jesus in you. If God answered all your prayers instantly, it would never develop patience in you. It would never develop long suffering in you. It would never develop the fruit of the spirit in you.

Not only that, it is necessary to stay focused because distractions are one of Satan's primary weapons which he uses against us in an attempt to keep us from having what God says belongs to us.

A distraction is anything that attempts to divert your attention. You could say it this way: Distractions are "focus thieves." That's why Solomon said in Proverbs 4:25, *Let thine eyes look right on, and let thine eyelids look straight before thee.*

Why do you need to look right on? Because if you don't, Satan will distract you.

Have you noticed that when you are believing for healing Satan will try to distract you by creating some other symptom in your body? Or, if you are believing for finances, Satan will try to distract you by something else breaking or not working. I call that symptoms of lack. I know what that's like. I have experienced it before.

Just about the time I found out God wanted me blessed and prosperous, the mailman showed up with another bill that I couldn't pay. Do you know what I am talking about?

Proverbs 4 in the Message translation says . . . *Keep your eyes straight ahead; and ignore all sideshow distractions . . .*

The sower soweth the word. And these are they by the way side, where the word is sown; but when they have heard, Satan comes immediately, and taketh away the word that was sown in their hearts. And these are they likewise which are sown on stony ground, who, when they have heard the word, immediately receive it with gladness; And have not root in themselves and so endure but for a time: afterward, when affliction or persecution ariseth up for the word's sake, immediately they are offended. And these are they which are sown among thorns; such as hear the word, and the cares of this world; and the deceitfulness of riches, and the lust of other things entering in, choke the word, and it becometh unfruitful.

– Mark 4:14-19

That's what Satan is after. He wants you to be unfruitful. He wants the Word to be unfruitful, non-productive, and producing no results in your life. That is what distractions are all about.

Distractions are designed by Satan to cause you to be unfruitful. That means that you won't get any results in your life and then you start blaming the Word or God for it when it had nothing at all to do with God and nothing at all to do with the Word. It was Satan using one of his best weapons against you. He got you distracted.

The book of James also tells us that distractions are designed by the devil to get you to become double-minded. What happens when a person becomes double-minded? When a person becomes double-minded that simply means that they are no longer focused, and usually it is because of a distraction.

For let not that man think that he shall receive any thing of the Lord. A double minded man is unstable in all his ways.

— James 1:7-8

So a double-minded man can't expect to receive anything from God. Why? Because he is unstable in all his ways. A double-minded man is a man who has lost his focus. This man has allowed distractions to come into his life, and those distractions have become focus thieves.

What do you do when you are faced with distractions? You stay focused on your vision. Smith Wigglesworth said, "I'm not moved by what I see. I'm not moved by what I feel. I'm not moved by what I hear. I'm moved only by what I believe, and I believe the Word of the Living God."

That needs to become your attitude when you are faced with distractions.

Satan is not going to just roll over and play dead because you have gotten a vision for living in the fullness of the blessing. No. He's not going to do that. Believe me. The fight will be on. He doesn't want you living the life that God has planned for you, but you have to determine to stay focused on your vision and not get distracted.

WRITE IT DOWN

"Well, how do I do that, Jerry?"

Habakkuk 2:2 says, *Write the vision and make it plain . . .* The Message translation says . . . *Write what you see . . .*

Every motivational book I have ever read has said somewhere in it, write your vision, write your goals, write your dream, write your objectives, write your plan.

Why is so important to write your vision down? Because writing it down and keeping it in front of you helps you to stay focused. And if you don't write it down, you are going to become easily distracted. But, you can always go back to what you wrote down, what you saw and what was revealed to you.

The Message translation goes on to say in Habakkuk 2 that *the vision message is a witness pointing to what's coming.* That's another reason it is so important to stay focused.

Your vision is future events that God wants manifesting in your life.

So let me ask you this: What is your testimony going to be? Is it going to be that you kept the faith, you didn't quit, you stayed focused and lived in the fullness of the blessing, or is your testimony going to be that you got distracted, gave up, and quit on your vision? Once again, vision enables you to stay focused. It enables you to see that there is something bigger on the inside of you than all of the negative circumstances that are going on around you.

VISION PRODUCES THE PERSEVERANCE THAT YOU NEED WHILE YOU ARE WAITING FOR YOUR VISION TO COME TO PASS

Visions generally don't come to pass overnight. That's why the Bible tells us in Habakkuk 2:3, *for the vision is yet for an appointed time . . . Though it tarry, wait for it . . . .*

Notice that God has already told us in advance not to get disappointed if it doesn't come to pass before dark. Though the vision tarries wait for it.

The dictionary defines *perseverance* as *the act of continuing a course in spite of difficulty, opposition, or adversity.* So that's what perseverance is. I like to call perseverance - outlasting the devil.

Now, Paul, he's my hero in the faith. I love this guy. Look at what he said:

And now behold, I go bound in the spirit unto Jerusalem, not knowing the things that shall befall me there. Save that the Holy Ghost witnesses in every city, saying that bonds and afflictions abide me, but none of these things move me . . .
– Acts 20:22

How can he say that? He just said that the Holy Spirit had already told him that when he gets to this next city, imprisonment, suffering, and affliction will be waiting on him. How do you face that and have the attitude that none of these things move me?

It was vision. What was on the inside of him was greater than what was happening on the outside. He went on to say, *I do not count my life dear to myself, that I might finish my course with joy.* Paul had a vision, and it was God-given. He had made up his mind that nothing he might go through was going to keep him from accomplishing what God told him to do nor keep him from having what God told him he could have.

That has to become your attitude about living in the fullness of the blessing. No matter how many bills you are faced with, no matter what shape your present car may be in, no matter the condition of the house you are living in right now, you have to be able to say: none of these things move me. Get a vision for living in the fullness of the blessing, and finish the course.

Paul's vision gave him the spiritual fortitude to "keep on keeping on" even in the midst of difficulty, opposition, and adversity. His vision propelled him. His vision motivated him. It inspired him and kept him going when everybody else would have given up. And your vision has to do the same for you.

If you will get a vision for living in the fullness of the blessing like God has always intended, and if you are willing to stay focused and persevere in the midst of opposition, I can tell you that it won't be long before your days of barely getting by will be over.

LET GOD BE GOD

Don't ask God how He is going to do it. That isn't any of your business and it is a waste of your time to try to figure it all out. Let God be God. He is the Most High God. He has ways that you could never dream up in a thousand years. You just do your part. Catch the vision and then let it ignite intense desire in your life, let it keep you focused, and keep you persevering. You do your part, and I promise that God will do His part.

CHAPTER 10

IT'S YOUR INHERITANCE

When my first grandchild was born, shortly after his birth, I took him in my arms. I looked down at him and said, "Grandson, I just want you to know, you picked the right family to be born into. Your grandmother and your grandfather are extremely blessed of the Lord, and as soon as I leave this hospital I'm going to go see my accountant, and I'm going to establish for you a trust fund and I will faithfully contribute to that trust fund every month, and by the time you're eighteen years old, it will provide for you a good life."

He was only 20 minutes old when I told him that. He couldn't even focus good yet. He did not know who I was and he certainly didn't understand what a trust fund was. But I did exactly what I told him I was going to do. I got in touch with my accountant, and we established the trust fund. I have contributed to it faithfully all these years.

Now, even though he didn't know what a trust fund was, it existed for him. He didn't have a clue what it was, but I had already arranged it for him.

For we are God's [own] handiwork (His workmanship), recreated in Christ Jesus, [born anew] that we may do those good works which God predestined (planned beforehand) for us[taking paths which He prepared ahead of time], that we should walk in them [living the good life which He prearranged and made ready for us to live].
– Ephesians 2:10 (Amplified version)

Paul is telling us that God has established something for us. He has established a trust fund for us so to speak, and He did it before the foundation of the earth.

God's trust fund for you is a good life, or you could say, living in the fullness of the blessing. Whether you understand what it is and what it involves or not, it exists.

Wouldn't you hate to think that you lived your whole life on this earth and somebody, like an uncle or somebody, had established a trust fund for you and you never knew about it and you never tapped into it?

Wouldn't you agree with me that you would have lived beneath your privileges?

What if I never told my grandson about his trust fund? What if I just went ahead and established it, contributed to it, and it continued to grow, and I never told him about it? What if I had died and he was never aware that his grandfather had established a trust fund for him? Then obviously he's going to live beneath his privileges. Right?

And that is the way most Christians live – beneath their privileges.

You have a trust fund. It has been established by God before you were ever conceived, and it's your inheritance. It's your right as a child of God.

Often when I would see my grandson, as he began to grow, I would talk to him about his trust fund. He still didn't understand what it meant. But by the time that he got to be five years old, he was calling me wanting to know how much interest it had earned. He was beginning to understand what this trust fund meant for his life. And by the time he was 18, he was "bugging" me about it all the time. He knew that he had a trust fund waiting for him, and he knew what it was going to mean for his life. It's the same with all my grandchildren now.

Their trust fund is waiting for them, and so is yours. The good life, living in the fullness of the blessing, has been waiting for you since the foundation of the earth. It exists. It is already there. You may not be able to see it in the natural realm, but it's there. You may not have experienced it yet, but it's there. He prearranged it.

LIVE THE GOOD LIFE

What is God's definition of the good life? It's found in Deuteronomy 28:1-13.

Now this is an exciting lifestyle that He is talking about.

And the Lord shall make you have a surplus of prosperity . . .
— Deuteronomy 28: 11 (Amplified version)

The definition for the word *surplus* is *over and above what is needed.*

That's the kind of life that God wants you to live. He does not want you living a life of barely getting by, just existing, living from paycheck to paycheck. That is not a blessed life in the mind of God. The blessed life in the mind of God is having a surplus of prosperity, and that is actually a characteristic of a blessed life.

As a child of God, it is your inheritance and your covenant right to be blessed coming in and going out. It is your right to be the head and not the tail, above and not beneath. Living in the fullness of the blessing is your right.

Because the Lord thy God shall bless thee in all thine increase, and in all the works of thine hands, therefore thou shalt surely rejoice.

– Deuteronomy 16:15

As a matter of fact, if you are not increasing, it is a violation of your covenant rights, and I would strongly suggest that you get fightin' mad at the devil today. Not at God, and not at anybody else. Get mad at the devil and declare a state of war on him.

HIS MOST PRIZED POSSESSION

What is man that thou art mindful of him? and the son of man, that thou visited him? For thou hast made him a little lower than the angels (a better rendering would be: a little lower than God) *and hast crowned him with glory and honor.*

– Psalm 8:4-5

Notice that God says man is His most prized possession, His most valuable creation. He said, "I've made him a little lower than myself." (author's paraphrase)

Creation will never be greater than the Creator, but you were made in His image, in His likeness. And He said there is something on your head. You may not be able to feel it.

You may not be able to see it. No one else may be able to see, but it's there. It's His glory and honor.

When you get up in the morning, you should be acting like a king. You ought to live like a king. You have been crowned with glory and honor. There's something on you – the blessing of God. It has marked your life, and it will bring increase in every area of your life.

Not only that, you are marked for the rest of your life. So don't sit around and let some devil talk you out of what belongs to you. God has pronounced His blessing on you and living in the fullness of that blessing rightfully belongs to you.

You have every right to say, "I'm blessed. I'm highly favored. Increase is on my life." The Bible says, *Let the redeemed of the Lord say so . . .* (Psalm 107:2).

If you will get up every day decreeing that you live in the fullness of the blessing of the Lord, then you will. The Bible says in Job 22:28, *Thou shalt decree a thing, and it shall be established unto thee . . .* So decree everyday, several times a day, that you live in the fullness of the blessing. Do it especially when the devil's trying to convince you that it isn't so.

WHY YOU NEED TO LIVE IN THE FULLNESS OF THE BLESSING

Why is it so important that you live in the fullness of the blessing? Why is it important that you should be increasing in every area of your life? For three reasons:

1) He wants you to increase so that you make Him look attractive to others.
2) He wants you to increase so that you can be a blessing and so that you can further the kingdom of God.
3) He wants you to increase so that you can finish the work of Jesus in the earth.

God said in Deuteronomy 8:18, *But thou shalt remember the Lord thy God: for it is he that giveth thee power to get wealth . . .* He has placed the blessing on you and all He is asking from you is to remember where it came from and what its real purpose is.

FIRST THINGS FIRST

But seek (aim at and strive after) first of all His kingdom and His righteousness, (His way of doing and being right), and then all these things taken together will be give you besides.

– Matthew 6:33 (Amplified)

So notice that you are to seek first, put as your priority and your number one pursuit, God's way of doing and being right. If you are ever going to live in the fullness of the blessing, then you have to make your number one priority seeking first God's way of doing things. He wants you to put Him first. Put His Word first. Put His way first place in your life.

What Jesus is actually saying is that if you will seek Him and His way first, then you won't have to pursue things, they will actually pursue you. They will chase you down. They will overtake you. If you will walk with God, the way He tells you to walk, then you are going to increase. Why? Because He has pronounced His blessing on your life. It's part of your covenant with Him. It's your trust fund that He has laid up for you.

To the person who has their priorities right, increase is going to come into their life. No devil will be able to stop it. Why? Because you have been blessed. And, as a result of being blessed, increase will come and God will bless that increase.

Do you know what happens when your increase is blessed? It becomes more and more. In other words, there is no end to it. God says that He will not only make you a blessing and bring increase into your life, but He will even bless your increase and He will cause living in the fullness of His blessing to be the story of your life.

Doesn't that sound like a good life? It is a good life. And God has it planned for you. God has placed the blessing on you. It has come to an explosive place. He is ready for you to live in the fullness of it, are you?

ABOUT THE AUTHOR

Dr. Jerry Savelle was an average, blue-collar man who was struggling and needed God's help. While he considered himself a "nobody," when he became a believer God told him not to worry about it because He was a master at making champions out of nobodies. God has since taken Dr. Savelle from being a constant quitter to a man who knows how to not give up and stand on the Word of God until victory is experienced. Because of the life-changing combination of God's faithfulness and Dr. Savelle's "no quit" attitude, his life is totally different than it was thirty-eight years ago. Known around the world for teaching people to win in life, Dr. Savelle founded Jerry Savelle Ministries International (JSMI), an organization dedicated to sharing God's message of love, acceptance, and hope across the globe. Since 1969, he has been actively motivating people to receive God's best. Dr. Savelle has ministered in more than three thousand churches and in twenty-six nations, and has overseas offices in the United Kingdom, Australia, Canada, and Africa.

God has used Dr. Savelle to impact people who are burned out on religion and who have backslidden in their walk with God, as well as Christians who have a need to hear the Word of God presented in terms applicable to their lives, dreams, and destinies. He is the host of a weekly television broadcast with his daughter, Terri, which airs in two hundred countries worldwide. Dr. Savelle is the author of more than forty books, including his best-sellers, *If Satan Can't Steal Your Joy, He Can't Keep Your Goods* and *You're Somebody Special to God*. He and his wife Carolyn also serve as founding Pastors of Heritage of Faith Christian Center in Crowley, Texas. They are the parents of two daughters, Jerriann and Terri, and they presently have seven grandchildren.

Other Books by Jerry Savelle

The Established Heart

Increase God's Way

Receive God's Best

Free to be Yourself

The God of the Breakthrough Will Visit Your House

If Satan Can't Steal Your Dreams, He Can't Control Your Destiny

Free at Last from Oppression

Free at Last from Old Habits

Thoughts – The Battle between Your Ears

Expect the Extraordinary

In the Footsteps of a Prophet

The Last Frontier

Take Charge of Your Financial Destiny

From Devastation to Restoration

Walking in Divine Favor

Turning Your Adversity into Victory

Honoring Your Heritage of Faith

Don't Let Go of Your Dreams

Faith Building Daily Devotionals

The Force of Joy

If Satan Can't Steal Your Joy, He Can't Keep Your Goods

A Right Mental Attitude

The Nature of Faith

Sharing Jesus Effectively

How to Overcome Financial Famine

You're Somebody Special to God

To order related material,
call, write, or visit our website
for further information.

Jerry Savelle Ministries
P.O. Box 748
Crowley, TX 76036
817-297-3155
www.jerrysavelle.org

For those who don't know Jesus, would you like to know Him?

If you were to die today, where would you spend eternity? If you have accepted Jesus Christ as your personal Lord and Savior, you can be assured that when you die, you will go directly into the presence of God in Heaven. If you have not accepted Jesus as your personal Lord and Savior, is there any reason why you can't make Jesus the Lord of your life right now? Please pray this prayer out loud, and as you do, pray with a sincere and trusting heart, and you will be born again.

Dear God in Heaven,

I come to You in the Name of Jesus to receive salvation and eternal life. I believe that Jesus is Your Son. I believe that He died on the cross for my sins, and that You raised Him from the dead. I receive Jesus now into my heart and make Him the Lord of my life. Jesus, come into my heart. I welcome You as my Lord and Savior. Father, I believe Your Word that says I am now saved. I confess with my mouth that I am saved and born again. I am now a child of God.